Miss Chao

Logic Posters, Problems & Puzzles

By Honi J. Bamberger

D1737698

SCHOLASTIC
PROFESSIONAL **B**OOKS

New York ▲ Toronto ▲ London ▲ Auckland ▲ Sydney ▲ Mexico City ▲ New Delhi ▲ Hong Kong

Dedication

This book is dedicated to my two daughters, Stephanie and Jessica. You have put up with your Mom spending far too much time with her work. While I do love what I do, I love the both of you more.

Cover design by Pamela Simmons and Jaime Lucero

Poster and interior illustrations by
Ellen Matlach Hassell, Manuel Rivera, and Rick Stromoski

Poster and interior design by Ellen Matlach Hassell
for Boultinghouse & Boultinghouse, Inc.

ISBN 0-590-64273-1

Printed in the U.S.A.

Contents

Acknowledgments 4

Introduction 5

Logic Posters **7**

Garden Poster Logic Problems. 10

Circle Graph Poster Logic Problems 13

Flag Poster Logic Problems 16

Money Poster Logic Problems 19

Number Logic and Arithmetic Logic Problems **22**

Number Logic Problems 25

Arithmetic Logic Problems 32

Logic With a Matrix **35**

Logic With a Matrix Problems 37

Logic Using a Venn Diagram **47**

Logic Using a Venn Diagram Problems 49

Answers 54

Acknowledgments

As I worked on this book I realized that my original love for solving logic problems with students began at the Park School, in Brooklandville, Maryland. I want to extend a special thanks to all of the fourth and fifth graders who inspired me to challenge them between the years 1978–1989. A thank you is also necessary to all of the students in K–3 (1990–1994) at New Hampshire Estates Elementary School in Silver Spring, Maryland. I created logic posters trying to come up with ways to reinforce mathematics vocabulary and motivate these children to think mathematically.

I would like to thank my daughter, Stephanie, for helping me type this manuscript when time was running out and a deadline had to be met. You have helped me so much this year!

I would also like to acknowledge all of the people at Scholastic Professional Books who have helped me put this book together. Terry Cooper first approached me and has believed in my ability to put my ideas on paper. Virginia Dooley inspired me to stick to a deadline and be sure that this book got completed. Thank you to everyone else who designed the cover, worked on the graphics, and made this book look so wonderful.

About the Author

Honi J. Bamberger, a former full-time classroom teacher, was one of three principal investigators from the University of Maryland who worked, from 1989–1995, with the teachers of Project IMPACT. She was a mathematics specialist offering ongoing support and teacher inservice to the teachers in this research study. She spent most of her time working in classrooms (Kindergarten–Grade Five) with students whose teachers participated in this study. In 1995 Dr. Bamberger joined the faculty at Johns Hopkins University as a research associate at the Center for Social Organization of Schools. Between 1995 and June 1997 she developed the first- and second-grade Math Wings program, and piloted it in twenty-five different classrooms across the country. Dr. Bamberger is currently the Executive Director of INSIGHT, a private center for research and mathematics staff development, in Columbia, Maryland.

Introduction

In 1989 the National Council of Teachers of Mathematics (NCTM) first disseminated its Curriculum and Evaluation Standards in an effort to help teachers better understand what mathematics content students needed to know to become mathematically literate citizens. Over the last ten years, mathematics teachers have shifted their mathematics program so that there was more of a balance between problem solving and computation, between concepts and skills, between independent activity and cooperative activity. Throughout the country teachers have embedded the four "process" standards (problem-solving, communication, reasoning, and connections) into their lesson plans as they think more reflectively about what children need to know and how children learn mathematics.

In the ten years since the NCTM Standards were first published, mathematics educators have continued to discuss what content and processes need to be used to enable all children to understand and use mathematics. As a result of these discussions Standards 2000 will have more developmentally appropriate categories (K–2, 3–5, 6–8, 9–12) and will include representation as one of its five process standards. The key content standards are condensed, and numeration, measurement, geometry and spatial reasoning, probability and statistics, and algebraic thinking are the areas to be taught to students.

The posters, puzzles, and problems in this book are meant to help students do several things:

▲ draw logical conclusions (which reinforces the reasoning standard),

▲ learn to justify their answers and solutions (which reinforces the reasoning standard),

▲ use different representations (diagrams, tables, Venn diagrams, and matrices) to organize and explain their thinking (which reinforces the new representation standard),

▲ reinforce various vocabulary terms that are used throughout mathematics (which reinforces both the communication and connections standard), and

▲ introduce and review concepts and skills that are taught in the intermediate grades (which reinforces each of the content standards listed above, in addition to problem solving)

Why Teach Logic in Math Class?

For all of the reasons that I've mentioned and then some. The problems foster communication in the classroom, both verbal and written. Using these puzzles and posters reinforces the important skills, concepts, and vocabulary that students tend to forget.

How to Get Started and When to Do These Activities

The different problems and puzzles in this book can be used to begin any mathematics lesson. They are a way to "turn on your students' minds"—to get them thinking. They can also be used outside of your regular math time in an effort to spend a bit more time reinforcing various mathematics vocabulary, skills, and concepts. Some teachers do "calendar" activities each morning. These puzzles fit in nicely with other daily routines. My students solved these logic problems while they waited to go home, when there was five minutes before lunch, or when someone was finished with an assignment and wanted to know, "What should I do now?" One year our school had so many snow days that we needed to extend the school day by fifteen minutes during the last month of school. We did a logic poster problem each afternoon.

The activities in this book work well as a whole-class activity, for independent centers, and for students to do while working in pairs.

The pages in this book have been designed so you can use them as reproducibles or with an overhead projector. Working through a problem while using an overhead projector is a great way to model how to solve these problems.

In addition to teaching logic, some of the concepts and skills covered in the book are listed in the chart on the right.

SKILL/CONCEPT
even and odd
prime and composite
sum, product, difference, factors, multiples
digit, number, numeral
ideas about square numbers and palindromic numbers
multiplicative arrays
greater than and less than
circle graphs
money
percent
sizes of angles (right, obtuse, acute)
common fractions and decimal fractions
place value
Venn diagrams and matrices
subtraction and addition (missing addends)

Logic Posters

Communication plays an important role in helping students make sense out of the many mathematics concepts, skills, and vocabulary that they are learning. Students build a meaningful understanding of mathematical ideas when they are actively involved in the process of learning. Colorful posters and activities that foster rich language experiences encourage students to participate fully in mathematical activities. In this way, the connections that students make are deep and long lasting. The colorful posters and accompanying logic problems encourage discussion, promote cooperative group work, and stimulate creative expression. They also give you a chance to model how to solve logic problems so students can work independently later.

I like to start these activities by displaying the poster and having students spend a few moments looking at it and thinking of different observations that they can make about it. Students should then brainstorm with each other and record some of these observations. Once students have had adequate time to look and then write or discuss, encourage them to share their observations with the rest of the class. It is likely that this part of the lesson will take as much as 30 minutes. No more than one or two logic problems should be given following this discussion. On subsequent days, you can use a poster-problem to begin the mathematics lesson.

Once all of the problems from one poster have been completed by your students, encourage them to generate their own problems, test them out to see if they work, and then give them to one another. A different poster can be used during each quarter of the school year, providing your students with many opportunities to review mathematics vocabulary and refine their reasoning skills.

The following teacher/students exchange (using the garden scene) demonstrates how a class might use these posters:

Teacher: Today we are going to use this poster to solve logic problems. Before we begin working, spend a minute looking at the poster. Think of different things that you can say about what you see.

Once students have had time to look and think, have them work with the people at their table (or in their group) and write down some of the observations. Give students about ten minutes to do this, or whatever amount of time seems appropriate. When students have completed this, have someone from the group share the observations. These papers can be displayed around the poster as a reminder of the class's observations. Some of the things that the students might say include:

Student: There are 4 gardens on the poster.

Student: Each garden has lots of vegetables.

Student: Each garden has rows of corn plants.

Student: There are 42 corn plants in Paulo's garden, 25 corn plants in Kim Yen's garden, 36 corn plants in Takani's garden, and 32 corn plants in Eric's garden.

Teacher: How did you figure out how many corn plants were in each of these gardens?

Student: I multiplied. Paulo has 7 corn plants going across and 6 going down. So, 7 times 6 equals 42. I did that for each of the gardens.

Student: You can do that for other vegetables too. Paulo has 6 cabbage plants. Takani has 7, Eric has 16, and Kim Yen has 11 that go around the perimeter of her garden.

Student: You could count all of the plants in each garden. I bet that some of the gardens have a total of more than one hundred plants.

Teacher: Well, maybe that's something that some of you would like to do. What are some other things that you can say about this poster?

Student: Each garden is different. Nobody has exactly the same amount of any kind of plant.

Student: Takani has the same amount of green peppers as Kim Yen has carrots. Both of them have 10.

It is likely that students will continue this discussion sharing all of the different things that they talked about in their group.

Teacher: I'm going to reveal the first clue and I want you to think about what it means and whether it describes one or more of the gardens. Don't raise your hand, just think about what the clue tells you. Then I'll give you time to talk with your partner about what you were thinking.

Reveal the first clue and read aloud: **This garden has an even number of corn plants.** Once students have had time to think and pair with their partners, ask them to share, out loud, what this clue tells them.

Student: This clue tells me that it could be Paulo's garden because he has 42 corn plants and 42 is an even number.

Student: It can't be Kim Yen's garden because she has 25 corn plants and 25 is an odd number.

Teacher: OK. What should we do to hide Kim Yen's garden so we don't think about it when we see some of the other clues?

Students may suggest crossing it out, covering it with a "Post-it," or putting a piece of paper over it. I find Post-its work best.

Student: It could also be Takani's or Eric's garden because Takani has 36 corn plants and that's an even number, and Eric has 32 corn plants and that's an even number also.

Teacher: So, the first clue tells us that Kim Yen's garden isn't the one that the clue is talking about but it could be any one of the other three. Let's look at the second clue. Just like before, first think about what it's telling you and then I'll give you time to talk about this with your partner.

Reveal the second clue and read aloud: **This garden has an amount of tomato plants that has factors of 2, 3, 4, and 6.** Give students time and then ask them to raise their hands to talk about what the clue tells them.

Student: It could be Paulo's garden because he has 12 tomato plants. All of those numbers are factors of 12.

Teacher: What do we mean when we say those numbers are factors of 12?

Student: It means that you can divide 12 by 2, 3, 4, or 6, and there won't be any remainder.

Student: It could also be Takani's garden. She has 24 tomato plants and that's another number that could be divided by 2, 3, 4, or 6 without any remainders.

Student: It can't be Eric's garden. He has 16 tomato plants. 2 is a factor of 16, and so is 4, but if you divide 16 by either 3 or 6 you'll

have a remainder. So we need to cover up Eric's garden too.

Teacher: Let's read the next clue and see if it tells us whose garden is being described.

Reveal the third clue and read aloud: **There are more carrots than green beans in this garden.** Give students time and then ask them to raise their hands to talk about what this clue tells them.

Student: Paulo has more carrots than green beans. He has 15 carrots and only 14 green beans.

Student: Well, Takani also has more carrots than green beans. She has 12 carrots and only 11 green beans.

Student: Both Takani and Paulo have 1 more carrot plant than green bean plant.

Student: This clue didn't help us figure out which garden is being described.

Teacher: Sometimes a clue isn't very helpful in figuring something out. Let's look at the next clue.

Read the fourth clue aloud: **There is an odd number of cabbage plants in this garden.**

Student: It can't be Paulo's garden because he has 6 cabbage plants and 6 is an even number. The garden being described has to be Takani's. She has 11 cabbage plants.

Garden Poster Logic Problems

1. ❧ This garden has an even number of corn plants.

   ❧ This garden has an amount of tomato plants that has factors of 2, 3, 4, and 6.

   ❧ There are more tomatoes than cabbages in this garden.

   ❧ There is an odd number of cabbage plants in this garden.

   Which garden is it? _____

2. ❧ This garden has an even number of tomato plants.

   ❧ This garden has an odd number of cabbage plants.

   ❧ The number of corn plants is a square number.

   ❧ If you divide the number of corn plants by 3, there will be a remainder of 1.

   Which garden is it? _____

3. ❧ There are more carrots than cucumbers in this garden.

   ❧ If you add the number of green pepper plants with the number of cabbage plants, the total is an odd number.

   ❧ The sum of the digits in the amount of tomato plants is a prime number.

   Which garden is it? _____

4. ❧ The quantity of green bean plants is an even number.

   ❧ 2 vegetables in this garden have the same amount of plants.

   ❧ The amount of carrots in this garden is a multiple of 3.

   ❧ If you subtract the amount of carrot plants from the amount of corn plants, the answer is 3^3.

   Which garden is it? _____

Garden Poster Logic Problems

5. ❧ If you add the number of green pepper plants with the number of cucumber plants, you get an even number greater than 20.

❧ There are more than 10 but less than 20 tomato plants.

❧ The number of green bean plants is an even number.

❧ If you divide the number of corn plants by the number of cabbage plants, the quotient is 7.

Which garden is it? _____

6. ❧ The cabbage plants are arranged in an array.

❧ The amount of space that the corn plants occupy is more than $\frac{1}{8}$ of the garden.

❧ There are more than $\frac{1}{2}$ dozen green pepper plants in the garden.

❧ The number of corn plants is the product of 12 and 3.

Which garden is it? _____

7. ❧ This garden has more corn than green peppers and cucumbers combined.

❧ This garden has more tomatoes than carrots.

❧ This garden has an odd number of green bean plants.

Which garden is it? _____

8. ❧ This garden was planted by a person who only plants things in rectangular arrays.

❧ This garden has an even number of green bean plants.

❧ This garden has an odd number of cabbage plants.

Which garden is it? _____

Garden Poster Logic Problems

9. ❧ This garden has an amount of vegetables that is the square root of 100.

❧ The number of corn plants in this garden is less than the product of 6 and 8.

❧ The number of corn plants in this garden is 5^2.

Which garden is it? _____

10. ❧ The number of tomato plants in this garden has 4 as one of its factors.

❧ There are more cucumbers than green pepper plants.

❧ This garden has more green bean plants than any other garden.

Which garden is it? _____

11. ❧ This garden has more than twice as many corn plants than cabbage plants.

❧ There are more green bean plants than cabbage plants.

❧ The number of green pepper plants is a multiple of both 2 and 5.

Which garden is it? _____

12. ❧ The corn plants in this garden occupy less than $\frac{1}{2}$ of the entire garden's space.

❧ This garden has fewer green bean plants than carrot plants.

❧ The difference between the number of corn plants and carrot plants is an odd number.

❧ There are fewer plants in this garden than any other garden.

Which garden is it? _____

Circle Graph Poster Logic Problems

1. ○ This graph shows that less than 30% of the money was saved.

○ This graph shows that more money was spent on snacks than on CDs or tapes.

○ If you combined the section of the graph that represents snacks with the amount that shows money saved, the total would be more than 50%.

○ This graph shows that 50% of students' money was either saved or was spent on CDs.

Which graph is it? _____

2. ○ This graph shows that 25% of the students' allowance was used to buy CDs.

○ On this graph more than 25% of their allowances was spent on snacks.

○ This graph shows that the smallest percentage of money was saved.

Which graph is it? _____

3. ○ This graph shows that more money was spent on CDs and tapes than was spent on video games.

○ This graph shows that less than 25% of the class's money was saved.

○ If you combined the amount of money used for snacks, video games, and also savings, it would still be less than the amount used to buy CDs and tapes.

Which graph is it? _____

4. ○ The average allowance for students in this class is $10.00 a week.

○ More than $2.50 is used to buy things.

○ Less than $5.00 is used to buy snacks.

○ Less than $2.50 is used to play video games.

○ The same amount of money is saved as is spent on CDs and tapes.

Which graph is it? _____

Circle Graph Poster Logic Problems

5. ◐ In this class graph there are no 90° angles for any one section.

◐ There is at least one obtuse angle when you look at this graph.

◐ Less money is used to buy snacks than was saved.

◐ The money saved combined with the money used to buy snacks is $\frac{1}{2}$ of the total area of the graph.

Which graph is it? _____

6. ◐ The angle showing the section used to buy snacks is an acute angle.

◐ The angle showing the section used to play video games is acute.

◐ The angle showing the section used for buying CDs or tapes is obtuse.

◐ The angle showing the section of saved money is obtuse.

Which graph is it? _____

7. ◐ More students bought snacks with their allowance than saved it.

◐ Less than half of the money was spent on playing video games.

◐ Exactly 25% of the money was used to buy CDs or tapes.

◐ The percent of money used to buy snacks is equal to the combined amount that was saved, used for video games, and used to buy CDs and tapes.

Which graph is it? _____

8. ◐ This graph has at least one section of it showing an acute angle.

◐ No section on this graph has a right angle.

◐ The amount of money saved, used to buy snacks, and to play video games is less than the amount used to purchase CDs.

Which graph is it? _____

 Logic Posters, Problems & Puzzles   Scholastic Professional Books

Circle Graph Poster Logic Problems

9. ◑ More than 25% of this class's money was spent on CDs, tapes, and video games.

◑ More than 25% of this class's money was spent on snacks.

◑ This class saved less than 25% of its money.

Which graph is it? _____

10. ◑ Only one part of this graph shows an acute angle.

◑ The acute angle is less than 50°.

◑ The part of the graph that shows the amount of money spent on snacks is more than 25% of the circle.

◑ The part of the graph that shows the amount of money spent on snacks is less than 50% of the circle.

Which graph is it? _____

11. ◑ The students in this teacher's class saved more money than they used to buy snacks.

◑ This teacher's class spent more than 25% of its money on CDs.

◑ This teacher's class spent more money on CDs than on snacks.

◑ From the graph it looks like the area that shows the money spent on CDs is twice the size of the area used to show the money spent on snacks.

Which graph is it? _____

12. ◑ Less than 50% of the class's money was spent on video games.

◑ The amount spent on CDs is more than 25% of the money.

◑ If you combined the amount spent on CDs, snacks, and video games it is more than 75% of the graph.

Which graph is it? _____

Flag Poster Logic Problems

1. ★This flag shows an even amount of stars.

   ★The stars on this flag are not in a rectangular array.

   ★If you added the digits in the year that this flag was displayed, the sum is less than 20.

   Which flag is it? _____

2. ★This flag has fewer white stripes than red stripes.

   ★The number of stripes on this flag is the same as $(7 \times 2) - 1$.

   ★The number of stars on this flag is a prime number.

   Which flag is it? _____

3. ★This flag has more than 15, but less than 7^2 stars on it.

   ★The flag has an even number of stars on it.

   ★The even number of stars that the flag has equals $(100 \div 5) + (4 \times 7)$.

   Which flag is it? _____

4. ★This flag has an even number of white stripes.

   ★If you combined the amount of stars with the amount of red stripes, the sum would be an odd number.

   ★There are more than 20, but less than 60 stars on this flag.

   ★You could not make the multiplication number sentence of $6 \times 8 = 48$ by looking at this flag.

   Which flag is it? _____

Flag Poster Logic Problems

5. ★The stripes on this flag produce an AB pattern.

★If you connected the stars around the perimeter, you would draw a rectangle.

★The stars are not in an array.

★If you drew diagonal lines through the stars, the pattern would be 1, 3, 5, 3, 1.

Which flag is it? _____

6. ★Half of the stars on this flag equals an even number.

★Twice the number of stars on this flag equals an even number less than 100.

★One-third of the stars on this flag equals 16.

Which flag is it? _____

7. ★This flag was created after the eighteenth century.

★If you added the amount of stars with the amount of stripes the sum would be more than 50.

★This flag shows the most stars.

Which flag is it? _____

8. ★The design created by the stars on this flag shows vertical symmetry.

★The design created by the stars on this flag shows horizontal symmetry.

★The line of symmetry runs through a row and also a column of stars.

★There are 5 stars on each side of the line of symmetry.

Which flag is it? _____

Flag Poster Logic Problems

9. ★The date of this flag is an odd number.

★The number of stars on this flag is greater than 2^3.

★The number of stars on this flag is 5 ($\sqrt{100}$).

Which flag is it? _____

10. ★If you subtract the total number of stripes from the number of stars, the difference is an odd number.

★The number of stars is an even number which is less than the product of 10 and 5.

★The number of stars on this flag is 7 more than the number of stars on the U.S. flag of 1777.

Which flag is it? _____

11. ★This flag does not have stars for Hawaii and Alaska.

★The difference between the number of stars and stripes on this flag is not 0.

★There are 8 columns of stars on this flag.

Which flag is it? _____

12. ★The sum of the digits in this flag's date is less than 25 but greater than 15.

★This flag was designed before Franklin D. Roosevelt was the President of the United States.

★This flag has 30 fewer stars than the flag of 1997.

Which flag is it? _____

Money Poster Logic Problems

1. $ This person's savings is more than $20.00.

   $ This person's savings has an even number of dimes and an even number of nickels.

   $ This person has 4 bills in his or her savings.

   $ This person has the same as 3 ten dollar bills, 2 one dollar bills, plus a quarter and a nickel.

   Which person is it? _____

2. $ This person does not have the most money in his or her savings.

   $ If you rounded this person's savings to the nearest $10.00, the amount would be $30.00.

   $ This person has 4 different coins in his or her savings.

   $ The total value of the coins is $2.82.

   Which person is it? _____

3. $ This person's savings shows more coins than bills.

   $ There are more dimes than pennies in this person's savings.

   $ There are an odd number of coins in this person's savings.

   Which person is it? _____

4. $ There is the same amount of bills as there is one kind of coin in this person's savings.

   $ The total value of nickels is $0.20.

   $ The value of nickels combined with dimes equals $0.60.

   Which person is it? _____

Money Poster Logic Problems

5. $ This person has an even amount of bills in his or her savings.

$ The total amount of the bills is more than $25.00.

$ This person has fewer than 15 coins.

$ The total value of this person's coins is less than $1.00.

Which person is it? _____

6. $ This person has more than 10 coins in savings.

$ The value of the dimes is greater than $0.50.

$ The sum of the quantity of nickels and pennies is an even number less than 8.

Which person is it? _____

7. $ This person has an even amount of coins.

$ This person has more than $30.00 in bills.

$ This person has $0.64 in coins.

Which person is it? _____

8. $ This person has saved less than $75.00.

$ This person has saved more than $25.00.

$ This person has fewer than 15 coins.

$ This person's coins total $2.82.

Which person is it? _____

Money Poster Logic Problems

9. $ This person has more coins than bills.

$ This person has more than 15 coins.

$ The total amount of money, in bills, is an odd number.

$ This person has less than $20.00 in bills.

Which person is it? _____

10. $ This person has more dimes than nickels.

$ This person's dimes total more than $0.50.

$ This person's coins total more than $1.00.

$ The total amount of money that this person has is more than $25.00.

Which person is it? _____

11. $ This person has at least one quarter.

$ This person's coins total more than $2.00 of the total amount of money.

$ This person has less than $30.00 saved.

$ The value of this person's quarters, nickels, and pennies is $0.82.

Which person is it? _____

12. $ This person has saved more money than Brandon.

$ This person has more coins than bills.

$ This person has more than $0.30 in dimes.

$ This person's dimes and nickels equal $1.00.

Which person is it? _____

Number Logic and Arithmetic Logic Problems

The logic problems that follow provide students with wonderful opportunities to improve their number sense and use arithmetic skills. The problems also give them a chance to use mathematics vocabulary in context. When vocabulary words are taught in isolation, students frequently forget their meaning and then are "stumped" when these words appear in word problems and on tests.

These problems can be done with an entire class as a warm-up to the mathematics lesson. They may also be used by students at a "center" or for independent seatwork.

My students used problems that I created as springboards to write their own number logic problems. The problems that they wrote were often far more difficult than any that I created.

Number Logic Problems

There are 25 number logic problems on pages 25–31. The first five problems have a two-digit number as the answer. The second five problems have a three-digit number as the answer. Problems 11–15 have four-digit numbers for answers. The problems in the fourth group have a five-digit number as the answer and the last five problems have a decimal fraction as the answer. When working together as a class, reveal only one clue at a time and have students suggest several possible correct answers for each clue, until the final clue reveals the one, correct answer.

Arithmetic Logic Problems

The problems on pages 32–34 provide students with arithmetic practice at the same time that they use their intuitive number sense and understanding about what happens to numbers when they are added, subtracted, multiplied, and divided. These are great to use as "openers" to your mathematics lesson, or they can be used for homework or "challenge" work. Many students like to make up their own problems once they have had opportunities to solve a variety of problems given to them by their teacher.

The following teacher/students exchange models how to "turn students' minds on" before your mathematics class begins.

Teacher: Today we will use clues to figure out the number that the clues are describing. As a clue is read, I will ask you to keep your hands down and think of a possible correct answer. You will have ten seconds to do this and then you will be given twenty seconds to share your answer with your partner. Once everyone has had a chance to do this, I will

WHAT IS THE NUMBER?

ask you to raise your hands so we can hear some of the answers that people came up with.

Reveal the first clue: **This number is a three-digit number.** Wait while students think and then whisper their answers to their partner. Then call on at least ten different students to share their answers. After a student responds say, **OK.** Then record their answer on the transparency or on chart paper.

Teacher: Could all of these answers be correct based on the clue that we have read? (*After a student answers, continue.*) What does it mean for a number to be a "three-digit number"?

Have several students respond. Then reveal the next clue: **This number is a multiple of ten.** Again, give the students about ten seconds to think and then have them whisper their answers to their partner. Call on several students to share their answer. *Notice how to respond to an incorrect answer.

Student 1: 300

Teacher: How did you know that this would be a correct answer?

Student 1: It's a three-digit number, and it's a multiple of 10.

Teacher: What does it mean to be a "multiple of 10"?

Student 1: It means that you can multiply something times 10 and you'd get the number. 30 times 10 equals 300.

Teacher: Can anyone else explain what a "multiple of 10" means?

Student 2: If you divide the number by 10 then you won't get a remainder. 10 goes into the number evenly. 300 divided by 10 is 30.

Teacher: What are some other possible correct answers that go with the first and second clues?

Student 3: 450

Student 4: 670

Teacher: How did you know that 670 would be correct?

Student 4: It's like what was said before. If you multiply 67 times 10, 670 is the product. You have to think: Is there a number which when multiplied by 10 will equal a three-digit number.

Teacher: OK. Are there any other numbers that would be correct ?

Student 5: 589

Teacher: How did you know that that would be a correct answer?

Student 5: It's a three-digit number.

Teacher: That's true for the first clue. What does the second clue tell us about the number.

Student 5: It has to be a multiple of 10.

Teacher: Is 589 a multiple of 10?

Student 5: I think so.

Teacher: What could you do to check?

If the student is unsure of what to do, ask one of the students who defined what is meant by a multiple of 10 to say what that means again. Then ask if there would be a remainder if you divided 589 by 10. If the student is unsure, do the computation with the class and show what occurs. Then ask if 589 is a multiple of 10. It is likely that the student will "change his or her mind." Then ask for several other numbers that would fit both clues before giving the next clue: **This number has only even digits.**

Student 1: 240

Student 2: 480

Student 3: 640

Student 4: 420

Teacher: How do we know that each of these is a possible correct answer?

Student 5: Each of the digits in each of the numbers is even.

Teacher: What is an even number?

Student 6: It's a number that can be split into two parts without any remainders.

Teacher: What are all of the even digits?

Student 7: Well, 2 splits into two 1s. 4 splits into two 2s. 6 splits into two 3s. 8 splits into two 4s. I guess that 0 splits into two 0s.

Student 8: Also, the even numbers are in a pattern. If you start counting, first there's one and that's odd. Then there's two and that's even. Then it's odd, even, odd, even… forever. So, if 1 is odd and the numbers on each side of an odd number are even, then 0 has to be even.

Teacher: Ok. Here's the next clue: **The digit in the hundreds place is 4 more than the digit in the tens place.**

Student 1: 620

Student 2: 400

Student 3: 840

Teacher: Are those the only possible correct answers now?

Student 4: Yes.

Teacher: Here is the last clue: **The digit in the tens place is 2 more than the digit in the ones place.**

Student 1: The answer has to be 620.

Once all students agree, return to the first clue and read each one making sure that the answer checks with each clue.

Number Logic Problems

Use the clues to find the number being described.

1. ♦ This two-digit number is less than 100.
   ♦ This number is odd.
   ♦ The sum of the digits in the ones place and tens place is 13.
   ♦ The number in the ones place is less than the number in the tens place.
   ♦ The number in the tens place is 2 less than 10.

   What is the number? _____

2. ♦ The number is between 10 and 100.
   ♦ The number is an even number less than 50.
   ♦ The sum of the digits in the ones place and tens place is the double of 5.
   ♦ The tens place digit is 2 less than the ones place digit.

   What is the number? _____

3. ♦ The number is greater than 10 but less than 100.
   ♦ The number is not prime; it is composite.
   ♦ The number is not a palindrome.
   ♦ The digit in the ones place is greater than the digit in the tens place.
   ♦ The sum of the two digits is 13.
   ♦ The product of the two digits is 40.

   What is the number? _____

4. ♦ This two-digit number is less than 100.
   ♦ The number is even.
   ♦ The number has 2, 3, and 4 as factors.
   ♦ The number is more than a dozen.
   ♦ The sum of the digits is 6.

   What is the number? _____

10

300

2,000

5

50,000

35

20

600

9

1,000

Number Logic Problems

Use the clues to find the number being described.

5. ◆ This two-digit number is a multiple of 10.
  ◆ The number is a multiple of 3.
  ◆ The number is not a multiple of 8.
  ◆ The number is a multiple of 9.
  ◆ The sum of its two digits equals 9.

  What is the number? _____

6. ◆ The number is between 1 and 1,000.
  ◆ Each of the three digits is different.
  ◆ Each digit is a square number.
  ◆ The difference between the digit in the hundreds and tens place is the quotient of 100 ÷ 20.
  ◆ The digit in the tens place is the largest of the digits.

  What is the number? _____

7. ◆ The number is a three-digit number that is less than 300.
  ◆ The sum of the digits in this number equals the number of months in one year.
  ◆ Each digit in this number is prime.
  ◆ The hundreds place is an even number.
  ◆ The digit in the ones place is the first odd prime number.
  ◆ The sum of the numbers in the hundreds and tens place is 9.

  What is the number? _____

8. ◆ The number is a three-digit number.
  ◆ The sum of the digits in this number is 16.
  ◆ The hundreds place has a number that is considered neither prime or composite.
  ◆ The number is a square number.

  What is the number? _____

10

300

2,000

5

50,000

35

20

600

9

1,000

Logic Posters, Problems & Puzzles Scholastic Professional Books

Number Logic Problems

Use the clues to find the number being described.

9. ◆ The number is a three-digit number.
   ◆ This number is a multiple of 5.
   ◆ There are no 0s in this number.
   ◆ The number in the hundreds place is one less than the number in the ones place.
   ◆ The number in the tens place is twice the amount of the digit in the hundreds place.

   What is the number? _____

10. ◆ The number is a three-digit number.
    ◆ The number is a multiple of 10.
    ◆ Each digit is less than 5.
    ◆ The number is greater than 100 but less than 500.
    ◆ The digit in the hundreds place is an even factor of 6.
    ◆ The digit in the tens place is an odd factor of 6.

    What is the number? _____

11. ◆ This is a four-digit number.
    ◆ It is greater than 2,000 but less than 6,000.
    ◆ There are only two different numerals used to make this number.
    ◆ The number is a multiple of 5.
    ◆ The number is not a multiple of 10.
    ◆ The digit in the thousands place is the same as the digit in the ones place.
    ◆ The sum of all four digits is 10.
    ◆ The number is a palindrome.

    What is the number? _____

10

300

2,000

5

50,000

35

20

600

9

1,000

Number Logic Problems

Use the clues to find the number being described.

12. ◆ This is an even number less than 10,000 but greater than 5,000.

◆ Two of the digits in this number are odd, and two of the digits are even.

◆ The sum of the even digits is 6.

◆ The sum of the odd digits is 1 less than 11.

◆ The even digits are in the ones place and hundreds place.

◆ The is a 2 in the hundreds place.

◆ The digit in the tens place is 1 more than the digit in the hundreds place.

What is the number? _____

13. ◆ The number is even.

◆ This is a four-place number with only three different digits.

◆ The digits in the ones and tens place are different.

◆ The digit in the ones place is a square number that is even.

◆ The digits in the thousands and hundreds place are square numbers that are odd and that sum to 2.

◆ The sum of all four digits is 11.

What is the number? _____

14. ◆ The number has four digits.

◆ Two of the digits are even numbers.

◆ The even numbers are in the ones place and thousands place.

◆ There is one 3 in the hundreds place.

◆ No digit, in the entire number, is greater than 5.

◆ No digit, in the entire number, is less than 2.

◆ The digit in the ones place is twice the digit in the thousands place.

◆ There are four different digits in this number.

What is the number? _____

10

300

2,000

5

50,000

35

20

600

9

7,000

Number Logic Problems

Use the clues to find the number being described.

15. ◆ This is an even number that has four digits.

◆ Only two different even numbers are used.

◆ The same digit is in the ones and tens place.

◆ The digit in the ones place is $\frac{1}{4}$ the digit in the thousands place.

◆ The two-digit number made by the tens and ones place is $\frac{1}{4}$ the two-digit number made by the thousands and hundreds place.

What is the number? _____

16. ◆ This number is between 10,000 and 20,000.

◆ This is an odd number.

◆ Each digit in this number is different

◆ Each digit in this number is odd.

◆ The digit in the ten thousands place is 8 less than the digit in the ones place.

◆ If you multiply the digits in the tens and thousands place the product is 35.

◆ The digit in the tens place is a factor of 10.

◆ The digit in the hundreds place is 4 less than the digit in the thousands place and 2 less than the digit in the tens place.

What is the number? _____

17. ◆ This five-digit number is greater than 50,000 but less than 99,999.

◆ Each digit in the number is a multiple of 3.

◆ There is only one 6 in the number.

◆ The 6 is in the ten thousands place.

◆ The two 9s in the number are between the 3 in the ones place and the 3 in the thousands place.

What is the number? _____

10

300

2,000

5

50,000

35

20

600

9

7,000

Number Logic Problems

Use the clues to find the number being described.

18. ◆ The number is between 20,000 and 100,000.

◆ Each digit is different, but there is no 1 in this number.

◆ The 0 in the hundreds place is the only even numeral in the number.

◆ The product of the digits in the ones and tens place is 15.

◆ If you looked at the two-digit number in the tens and ones place it would be the prime number between 50 and 55.

◆ The digit in the tens thousands place is 6 more than the digit in the ones place.

What is the number? _____

19. ◆ This number has five digits, and no digit is greater than 4.

◆ It is between 20,000 and 30,000.

◆ The 4 is in the thousands place. All but one of the digits is even.

◆ The digit in the hundreds place is 3 less than the digit in the thousands place.

◆ The sum of all five digits is 7.

What is the number? _____

20. ◆ This five-digit number is a palindrome.

◆ There is a 0 in the tens place.

◆ There is a 4 in the ten thousands place.

◆ The digit in the hundreds place is 1 less than the digit in the ones place.

What is the number? _____

21. ◆ This number is between 0 and 1.

◆ This decimal fraction is a way to show the value of one of the coins used in the United States.

◆ This decimal fraction shows an amount that is more than a nickel but less than a half dollar.

◆ This decimal shows $\frac{1}{4}$.

What is the number? _____

Number Logic Problems

Use the clues to find the number being described.

22. ♦ This decimal fraction is more than $\frac{1}{4}$ but less than 1.
    ♦ This decimal fraction is more than $\frac{4}{5}$.
    ♦ This decimal fraction is between .81 and .91.
    ♦ This decimal fraction has only one place.

    What is the number? _____

23. ♦ This number is between 0 and 1.
    ♦ This decimal fraction is less than $\frac{1}{4}$ but more than $\frac{1}{10}$.
    ♦ This decimal fraction has three digits.
    ♦ There is a 1 in the tenths place of this decimal fraction.
    ♦ This decimal fraction is between .16 and .17.
    ♦ The sum of all three digits of this decimal fraction is 16.

    What is the number? _____

24. ♦ The number is between $\frac{1}{4}$ and $\frac{1}{2}$.
    ♦ The number is a two-digit decimal fraction.
    ♦ Both digits of this number are even.
    ♦ Neither digit is a 6 or a 2.
    ♦ The digit in the tenths place is $\frac{1}{2}$ the digit in the hundredths place.

    What is the number? _____

25. ♦ This number is between 0 and $\frac{3}{4}$.
    ♦ This decimal number has three places.
    ♦ This decimal number is less than $\frac{1}{10}$.
    ♦ This decimal number is between $\frac{6}{100}$ and $\frac{7}{100}$.
    ♦ The digits 6 and 7 are in this decimal number.

    What is the number? _____

10

300

2,000

5

50,000

35

20

600

9

1,000

Arithmetic Logic Problems

Use any combination and or any quantity of +, −, ×, and ÷ signs to make each expression true. There may be more than one correct answer.

1. 4   3   2   1 = 6

2. (9   2)   6   1 = 4

3. (7   9)   4   3 = 1

4. [(8   4)   3]   4 = 2

5. (1   2)   4   3 = 9

6. [(3   8)   7]   2 = 8

7. 12   3   9   8 = 12

8. [(15   3)   4]   7 = 7

9. 1   4   6   8 = 3

10. 2   2   2   2 = 6

Name _____

Arithmetic Logic Problems

Use any combination and or any quantity of +, −, ×, and ÷ signs to make each expression true. There may be more than one correct answer.

11. (40   10)   2   30 = 70

12. 20   10   60   20 = 90

13. 90   2   5   1 = 10

14. 60   4   5   5 = 15

15. 6   5   2   10 = 50

16. 12   8   20   5 = 35

17. 55   2   10   20 = 120

18. 75   25   15   10 = 55

19. 80   8   2   2 = 40

20. 10   10   20   15 = 20

Arithmetic Logic Problems

Use any combination and or any quantity of +, −, ×, and ÷ signs to make each expression true. There may be more than one correct answer.

21. $(136 \quad 20) \quad 2 \quad 100 = 132$

22. $51 \quad 3 \quad 12 \quad 1 = 28$

23. $164 \quad 4 \quad 2 \quad 27 = 109$

24. $88 \quad 2 \quad 4 \quad 10 = 34$

25. $100 \quad 5 \quad 35 \quad 7 = 48$

26. $(0.75 \quad 0.30) \quad 2 \quad 0.10 = 1.00$

27. $\frac{1}{2} \quad \frac{1}{6} \quad \frac{1}{5} = \frac{8}{15}$

28. $2 \quad \frac{9}{10} \quad 1\frac{1}{3} = \frac{7}{15}$

29. $4 \quad 0.25 \quad 0.10 \quad \frac{1}{2} = 0.6$

30. $[(\frac{2}{3} \quad \frac{1}{2}) \quad \frac{1}{4}] \quad 2 = 1\frac{5}{6}$

Logic With a Matrix

Using a matrix to organize information is a great way to solve certain logic problems. A matrix helps students isolate the information that is helpful in solving the problem and eliminate the information that is no longer needed. Logic problems that have three variables have a very different looking matrix. Without this visual representation, information is difficult to remember and consequently difficult for students to use.

The following is a teacher/students exchange from a fifth-grade classroom where students are solving the first problem in this section of the book.

Teacher: Today we are solving a different kind of logic problem and will use something called a matrix to help us solve it.

Show students the first problem and the matrix and ask them to tell you what they see.

Student: The matrix is like a square with different parts.

Student: There are names across the top of the matrix and different kinds of drinks along the side.

Student: The squares in the middle are empty.

Teacher: Will someone read the logic problem and then I'll read one clue at a time and we can use the matrix to solve it.

Have a student read the problem out loud and then read the first clue.

Student: What does it mean that Jamie and Sandy are good friends? What does that have to do with which drink they like best?

Teacher: Does anyone think they know how this clue helps us solve the problem?

Student: I think that it means that Jamie and Sandy can't be the people who like skim milk the best because they are friends with that person. So Jessie has to be the person who likes skim milk the best. Jamie and Sandy are good friends with Jessie who likes skim milk the best.

Teacher: Does that make sense to all of you? What can we put in the matrix to help us remember that it's Jessie who likes skim milk the best? We also need to put something in the matrix to help us remember that Sandy and Jamie do not like skim milk the best.

Student: You could put a check where Jessie and skim milk come together and then put an × in the same row under Sandy and Jamie.

Student: Or you could color in the place to show that Jessie is the skim-milk person and put an × under Sandy and Jamie.

Student: You also need to show that Jessie can't like any of the other drinks the best. So you'll need to draw ×'s underneath Jessie's name.

Teacher: Why don't I color in the place where it shows that Jessie likes skim milk the best?

Then it will be easy to see that Jessie is the skim-milk person. I'll put ×'s to show that no other person can have skim milk as their favorite drink, and to show that Jessie cannot like any of the other drinks as his favorite. The next clue says, **Sandy likes a beverage that has an odd number of letters.** Take ten seconds to think about this and then whisper what you think to your partner.

Once students have had this time, call on several students to share their ideas.

Student: Spring water and orange juice both have an odd number of letters. There's eleven letters in both of these drinks.

Teacher: So, what does that mean?

Student: It means that we still don't know which person likes which drink the best.

Teacher: OK. Let's read the next clue. **Jamie does not like fruit juices.** What does this clue tell us?

Student: This means that Jamie can't like orange juice. Orange juice is a fruit juice.

Teacher: So, what do I need to do on the matrix?

Student: You need to put an × where it shows Jamie and orange juice. Then you can color in where it shows Jamie and spring water. If he doesn't like orange juice the best, then he has to like spring water the best.

Teacher: OK. Now do we know which beverage Sandy likes the best?

Student: When you put an × under Jamie and orange juice that just leaves Sandy and orange juice. So, Sandy likes orange juice the best. Color in that square.

Teacher: Let's look at the matrix and see if it shows us who likes which beverage the best. You'll need to record your answers so it's easier to see them. Look over the matrix and reread the clues, checking to see that the answers make sense.

The 18 logic problems that follow include matrices for students to use to solve them.

Logic With a Matrix

Use the matrices to solve the problems.

1. Sandy, Jamie, and Jessie each have a different favorite beverage. The drinks are skim milk, orange juice, and spring water. Use the clues to figure out which beverage is liked best by each person.

   • Jamie and Sandy are good friends with the person who likes skim milk.

   • Sandy likes a beverage that has an odd number of letters.

   • Jamie does not like fruit juices.

	Sandy	Jamie	Jessie
Skim milk			
Orange juice			
Spring water			

2. MaryBeth, Elizabeth, and Beth are all good friends, partly because they each have the name *Beth* in their names. They each have an unusual pet. One has a chameleon, one has a python, and one has a parrot. Use the clues to figure out which girl has which pet.

   • The person with the most letters in her name has the pet with the double letters in its name.

   • Beth and Elizabeth went over to the house of the girl who owns the python.

	MaryBeth	Elizabeth	Beth
Chameleon			
Python			
Parrot			

Logic With a Matrix

Use the matrices to solve the problems.

3. Melissa, John, and Chau wrote story problems for math class. These were the story problems that were written:

- Warren had 215 baseball cards in his collection. He gave 78 to his friend. How many cards does Warren have now?

- Evelyn planted corn in her garden. She planted 11 rows and there were 12 plants in each of these rows. How many plants did Evelyn have?

- Matilda had 350 pages in the biography that she was reading. She decided that she would read 35 pages a day. How many days will it take for Matilda to finish her book?

Use the clues to figure out which student wrote which problem.

- Melissa's problem was the only one that had an answer that was odd.

- John's problem has a two-digit number as the answer.

	Melissa	John	Chau
Warren problem			
Evelyn problem			
Matilda problem			

4. Doug, Matt, Jonah, and Jenny all grew up in the same town on the same street and went to the same elementary school. However, each person had a different fifth-grade teacher. The teacher's names were Ms. Parsons, Dr. Saunders, Mr. London, and Ms. Carr. Use the clues to figure out which teacher each person had.

- Matt did not have a female teacher.

- Dr. Saunders had her classroom in a portable because there wasn't enough room in the building.

- Jenny's teacher is a good friend of both Ms. Carr and Dr. Saunders.

- Doug Saunder's mother is Jonah's teacher.

	Doug	Matt	Jonah	Jenny
Ms. Parsons				
Dr. Saunders				
Mr. London				
Ms. Carr				

Logic Posters, Problems & Puzzles Scholastic Professional Books

Logic With a Matrix

Use the matrices to solve the problems.

5. Bernice, Florence, Walter, and Sharna collected data about the places where different classes of students liked to swim. Bernice surveyed the first-graders, Florence surveyed the second-graders, Walter surveyed the third-graders, and Sharna surveyed her classmates in fourth grade. Each grade level liked a different place to swim. The places were: the ocean, a lake, a swimming pool, and a pond. Use the clues to figure out which grade preferred which place to swim.

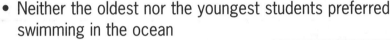

- Neither the oldest nor the youngest students preferred swimming in the ocean
- The students who liked swimming in the lake best, ate lunch each day with the third and second graders.
- The students Sharna surveyed like the lake the best.
- Second graders did not prefer the ocean or a swimming pool.
- The youngest children liked the pool the best.

	Bernice Grade 1	Florence Grade 2	Walter Grade 3	Sharna Grade 4
Ocean				
Lake				
Swimming Pool				
Pond				

6. Peter, Janice, Andrew, and Samuel love movies. One loves science-fiction films, one loves dramas, one loves comedies, and one loves westerns. Use the clues to figure out which person loves each type of movie.

- Andrew and Samuel don't like dramas.
- The girl loves science fiction.
- Andrew doesn't like westerns.

	Peter	Janice	Andrew	Samuel
Science Fiction				
Drama				
Comedy				
Westerns				

Logic With a Matrix

Use the matrices to solve the problems.

7. Marie, Brian, Sally, Freddie, and Patricia went on a bike trail together. Each one rode a different distance. The distances were: 5 kilometers, 7 kilometers, 10 kilometers, 11 kilometers, and 12 kilometers. Use the clues to figure out which person rode which distance.

   - Brian and the boy who rode 11 kilometers are good friends.
   - Sally rode exactly twice as many kilometers as Patricia.
   - Marie rode 5 more kilometers than Brian.

	Marie	Brian	Sally	Freddie	Patricia
5 km					
7 km					
10 km					
11 km					
12 km					

8. Gordon, Candi, Nikki, and Stefanie each spent a different amount of time completing their homework the first week of school. One spent 5 hours and 20 minutes. One spent 4 hours and 40 minutes. One spent 3 hours and 45 minutes, and one spent 6 hours and 15 minutes. Use the clues to figure out how much time each person spent on their homework the first week of school.

   - If you rounded the number of minutes that Gordon spent on his homework to the nearest hundred, it would be 300 minutes.
   - Gordon spent more time than Nikki on homework.
   - Stefanie spent 320 minutes on her homework.

	Gordon	Candi	Nikki	Stefanie
5 hours 20 min.				
4 hours 40 min.				
3 hours 45 min.				
6 hours 15 min.				

Logic With a Matrix

Use the matrices to solve the problems.

9. Five girls—Chau, Melinda, Hannah, Petra, and Benita—visited an amusement park. At the end of the day each said that they had a different favorite ride. These rides were named: Wild Grizzly, Tilt-a-Whirl, Mountain Climb, Swamp Coaster, and Ferris Wheel. Read the clues to figure out which ride was the favorite of each girl.

- Chau's favorite ride has 9 more letters in it than her first name.
- Melinda's favorite ride has 4 less letters than double the number of letters in her first name.
- Petra and Benita each love a ride that has 11 letters in its name.
- Benita's best friend loved the Ferris Wheel the best.

	Chau	Melinda	Hannah	Petra	Benita
Wild Grizzly					
Tilt-a-Whirl					
Mountain Climb					
Swamp Coaster					
Ferris Wheel					

10. Four friends talked about what they want to be when they become adults. Their names are Camille, Josie, Beth, and Mike. Each person wants to be something different. One wants to be an attorney, one wants to be an accountant, one wants to be a teacher, and one wants to work in a salon. Use the clues to figure out what each friend wants to become.

- The person who wants to become an accountant has the longest name.
- Josie and Mike were surprised when their friend said she wants to work in a salon.
- Josie doesn't want to work in a school.

	Camille	Josie	Beth	Mike
Attorney				
Accountant				
Teacher				
Salon				

Logic With a Matrix

Use the matrices to solve the problems.

11. *Charlie and the Chocolate Factory* by Roald Dahl, *Stuart Little* by E. B. White, *A Wrinkle in Time* by Madeline L'Engle, and *Tales of a Fourth Grade Nothing* by Judy Blume are the favorite books of Serena, Matthew, Jacob, and Dexter. Use the clues below to figure out which person loves which book.

   - Matthew's favorite book is written by a female author.
   - Neither Jacob nor Serena like books about animals.
   - Serena's favorite book is also about her favorite food.
   - Jacob hasn't read *A Swiftly Tilting Planet* which was also written by the author who wrote his favorite book.

	Serena	Matthew	Jacob	Dexter
Charlie and the Chocolate Factory				
Stuart Little				
A Wrinkle in Time				
Tales of a Fourth Grade Nothing				

12. Five children found out that their birthdays were all one day after a holiday. The children's names are Felicity, Monroe, Belinda, Wyatt, and Brook. Their birthdays are January 2, February 15, March 18, July 5, and December 26.

   Use the clues below to figure out each person's birthday.

   - Belinda's birthday is the only summer birthday.
   - Felicity's birthday comes right before New Year's Eve.
   - On his birthday, Wyatt's gifts are often wrapped in leftover Valentine's Day wrapping paper.
   - Monroe was almost the first baby born in the New Year.

	Felicity	Monroe	Belinda	Wyatt	Brook
January 2					
February 15					
March 18					
July 5					
December 26					

Name _____

Logic With a Matrix

Use the matrices to solve the problems.

13. Brian, Henry, Ernest, Chris, and Peter each wrote a different addition problem to challenge their friends. The problems that they wrote were 479 + 1,356=; 4,782 + 999=; 508 + 948=; 1,644 + 777=; and 827 + 699=. Use the clues below to determine which child wrote which problem.

- Ernest chose his problem because it has a sum that is even and the words *even* and *Ernest* both begin with an *e*.
- The sum for Chris's problem is less than Ernest's sum.
- Brian and Henry ate lunch with the boy who had the smallest, odd sum.
- If you rounded Brian's sum to the nearest thousand it would be 6,000.

	Brian	Henry	Ernest	Chris	Peter
479 + 1,356 =					
4,782 + 999 =					
508 + 948 =					
1,644 + 777 =					
827 + 699 =					

14. Julie, Kim, J.M., Robbie, Matt, and David collected data and represented it with the bar graph shown. Use the clues to figure out how to label the horizontal axis of this bar graph.

- Robbie and Julie rolled a six an even amount of times.
- Matt, David, and Kim were surprised when their friend rolled a six more than anyone else.
- Kim rolled a six two fewer times than J.M.
- If you add Matt's rolls of six to J.M's. rolls of six, the sum is 18.
- If you subtract Robbie's rolls of six from David's rolls of six, the difference is 3.

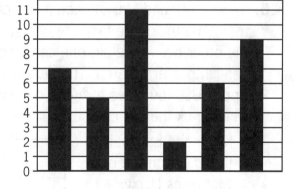

	Julie	Kim	J.M.	Robbie	Matt	David
7						
5						
11						
2						
6						
9						

Logic With a Matrix

Use the matrices to solve the problems.

15. Four fifth-graders—Mikhael, Sondrah, Charleen, and Yolanda—compared their home telephone numbers. Use the clues to determine which student has which telephone number.

- Sondrah and Yolanda both have a telephone number whose digits sum to 31.
- If you subtract the sum of the first three digits of Mikhael's telephone number from the sum of the second four digits of his number, the difference is 17.
- Sondrah's telephone number has only two even digits.

	Mikhael	Sondrah	Charleen	Yolanda
817-3624				
356-1178				
523-8199				
631-2140				

16. Kevin, Earl, and Marvin each has a pet that can do a special trick. The tricks are that one can stand on only two legs with the other two in the air, one can jump through a hoop, and one can jump over a barrel. The pets' names are Harry, Bozo, and Sport. Use the clues to figure out which boy has which pet and which trick the pet can do.

- Kevin and Earl walk to the mall with the boy who owns Harry.
- Bozo's owner has the same number of letters in his name as his pet does.
- Sport cannot jump.
- Marvin's pet can jump through things but not over things.

	Kevin	Earl	Marvin	Standing	Jumping hoop	Jumping barrel
Harry						
Bozo						
Sport						
Standing						
Jumping hoop						
Jumping barrel						

Logic With a Matrix

Use the matrix to solve the problem.

17. Wanda, Rita, Barbara, and Greta each wore a university sweatshirt. The sweatshirt colors that they wore were white, red, blue, and green. The names on the shirts were Washington State University, Rhode Island State University, Brown University, and Georgetown University. No two sweatshirts were the same color or had the same name on it. Use the clues below to figure out who wore which color sweatshirt and which name is on each sweatshirt.

- No person's shirt had a color or a name with the same letter as the person's name.
- Rita and Greta are friends with the girl who wore the red Washington State University sweatshirt.
- Wanda does not like the colors green and white.
- Rita's green shirt has the fewest number of letters on it.
- Rita's Brown University sweatshirt is not white.

	Wanda	Rita	Barb	Greta	White	Red	Blue	Green
Washington State								
Rhode Island								
Brown								
Georgetown								
White								
Red								
Blue								
Green								

Name _____

Logic With a Matrix

Use the matrix to solve the problem.

18. During her eight-week summer vacation, Amber traveled to a different city each week. The cities she visited were Seattle, Denver, Kansas City, Omaha, Charlotte, Baltimore, Atlanta, and Washington, D.C. Use the clues to figure out which city she visited each week of her vacation.

- Amber began her trip by visiting the city which is about 50 miles north of Washington, D.C.

- Amber did not go to Washington during the second week of vacation. Instead she flew to Georgia.

- She visited the White House during her fourth week of vacation.

- On the third week of her vacation, Amber visited the city that is in the same state as Greensboro and Raleigh.

- Amber visited Omaha after going to Charlotte, but not before spending time in Kansas City.

- During the seventh week, Amber traveled all the way to the west coast before visiting her Uncle Sydney in Denver.

	1st	2nd	3rd	4th	5th	6th	7th	8th
Atlanta								
Baltimore								
Charlotte								
Denver								
Kansas City								
Omaha								
Seattle								
Washington, DC								

Logic Posters, Problems & Puzzles   Scholastic Professional Books

Logic Using a Venn Diagram

Venn diagrams, developed by Englishman John Venn (1834–1923) are a powerful problem-solving tool allowing students to display attributes or information from two or three different sets. Teachers often use this visual representation when discussing the characters in a piece of literature or when making observations about things in science class. The Venn diagram logic problems that follow provide students with problems where they will have to add and/or subtract to figure out answers. In most cases the Venn diagram provides them with a means of seeing how the information from the problem will look.

The following is a teacher/students exchange from a sixth-grade classroom. This will help you see how to use these problems with your own students.

Teacher: Think of something you can say about this.

Show students the Venn diagram and ask them to describe what they see.

Student: There are two ovals that cross over each other.

Student: The ovals are empty.

Teacher: Has anyone ever used one of these before, or seen one of these?

Student: We use these to write characteristics of characters in a book. Sometimes two characters have characteristics that are the same and you write those in the middle part.

Student: The middle part means that the information is the same for both of the characters.

Teacher: Has anyone used these in any other classes?

Student: We used them in math class in third grade when we did data collection.

Teacher: So, this diagram has a special name. It's called a Venn diagram. It's actually named after a man named John Venn who used these to solve logic problems. We're going to use them to solve logic problems, too.

Show the first logic problem to the students and ask them to silently read the information that is given to them.

Teacher: Let's label the two ovals to help us organize the information from the problem. Think about what this *(Point to the first oval.)* might have as its label.

Student: You need to write the name of one of the favorite flavors of ice cream on top of each of the ovals.

Teacher: So, this loop will represent the students who like fudge swirl as their favorite flavor of ice cream and this oval will represent the students who like chocolate chip as their favorite flavor.

Add the labels.

Student: It says that 5 children only liked chocolate chip.

Teacher: Where should we write the number *5* to show that this amount of people only liked chocolate chip?

Student: You need to put it inside the loop that says *chocolate chip* in the part that doesn't overlap with the *fudge swirl* loop.

Teacher: How did you know that this would be the best place to put the *5*?

Student: The overlapping part would be for people who couldn't make up their mind, and they said that they liked both chocolate chip and fudge swirl the same.

Teacher: OK. Would someone read the next clue?

Student: 8 children only liked fudge ripple.

Teacher: So, where should we write the number *8?*

Student: The *8* needs to be inside the other loop in the part that doesn't overlap.

Student: 8 people liked only one kind of ice cream best.

Teacher: Would someone read the next statement?

Student: Some children liked them both the same.

Teacher: What do we know from this clue?

Student: We know that there needs to be a number in the middle, but we don't know what this number is yet.

Teacher: Let's look at the last clue and see if it helps us figure out how many students will need to go in the center. Would someone read the last clue?

Student: 22 children were surveyed.

Teacher: Talk with your partner and take a minute to figure out how many people will go in the intersection of the two loops.

Give children a minute to do this. After someone has given an answer be sure to ask them how they figured out the answer they shared.

Student: The number *9* has to go in the center.

Teacher: Did anyone get a different answer?

Teacher: How do you know that *9* is the correct amount?

Student: If you add the 5 and the 8 that equals 13. But the last clue says that a total of 22 students were surveyed. So, I subtracted 13 from 22 and that equals 9. So, 9 students liked both chocolate chip and fudge swirl the same.

The following Venn diagram problems can be used as a "warm-up" before beginning mathematics class or they can be used as independent work or paired work for students.

Name _____

Logic Using a Venn Diagram

Use the Venn diagrams to display the results in each problem.

1. Sara surveyed a group of fourth-graders to find out their favorite flavor of ice cream. They were given the choice of fudge swirl or chocolate chip. Here are the results.

   • 5 children only liked chocolate chip.

   • 8 children only liked fudge ripple.

   • Some children liked them both the same.

   • 22 children were surveyed.

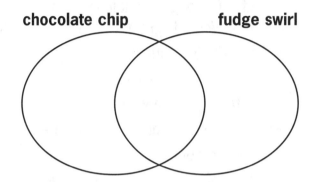

2. The entire fifth grade signed up for after-school sports. They signed up for soccer in the fall, basketball in the winter, and softball in the spring. Use the Venn diagram to display the data that was collected.

   • 50 signed up for soccer, 60 students signed up for basketball, and 52 signed up for softball.

   • A total of 112 students are in the fifth-grade.

   • Some students signed up for more than one sport.

   • 8 students signed up for all three sports.

   • 11 students signed up for softball and basketball only.

   • 7 students signed up for soccer and softball only.

   • 16 students signed up for soccer and basketball only.

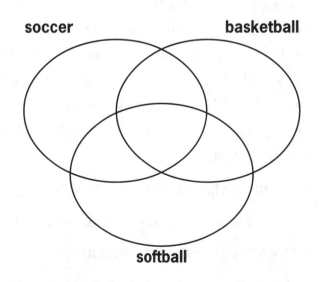

Name _____

Logic Using a Venn Diagram

Use the Venn diagrams to display these results and answer the questions.

3. Marvin stood outside of a pet shop every Saturday during the month of December to find out what types of pets were being bought as holiday gifts. He represented his data in a Venn diagram. Here is what he found.

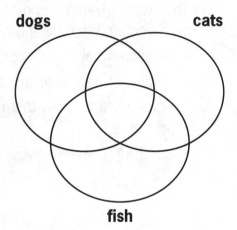

- A total of 33 dogs were bought.
- A total of 28 cats were bought.
- A total of 28 fish were bought.
- 12 people bought one of each pet.
- 2 people bought a cat and a dog.
- 10 people came out of the store without a pet.
- 3 people bought only fish.
- 8 people bought only cats.

How many people bought a dog and a fish? _____

How many people bought a cat and a fish? _____

4. After their summer vacation, 88 students were asked to share where they went.

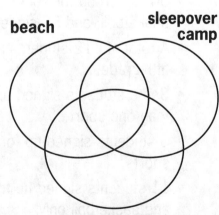

- 2 students spent four weeks at sleepover camp and then went to the beach for a week and then went hiking in the mountains for another week.
- A total of 34 students went to camp.
- 11 students went to both camp and the beach.
- 5 students went to the mountains and also to camp.
- A total of 12 students went to the mountains.
- 1 student vacationed at the beach and the mountains.
- 25 students went to the beach.

How many students stayed home? _____

How many students only went to the beach? _____

How many students only went to camp _____

How many students only went to the mountains? _____

Logic Using a Venn Diagram

Use the Venn diagrams to display the results in each problem.

5. Preparing for their class graduation party, 68 students voted on what food they wanted to serve. The choices they selected were pizza, subs, and hamburgers. Some students chose more than one food.

- 20 people picked only pizza but 36 people picked pizza.
- 29 people wanted subs.
- 4 of the students picked all three things.
- 11 students wanted burgers and subs.
- 7 students wanted subs and pizza.
- 30 people picked burgers.

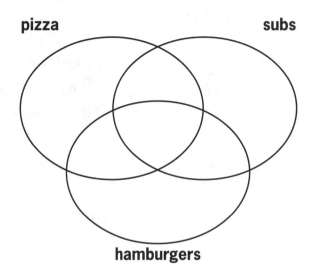

6. 100 dentists were surveyed about the toothpaste they recommended to their patients. The toothpastes were Sureshine, Mint-o, and Blast. Some of the dentists picked more than one toothpaste.

- 20 dentists recommended all three toothpastes.
- 30 recommended both Sureshine and Mint-o.
- 15 recommended only Mint-o.
- Mint-o was recommended by a total of 47 dentists.
- 26 recommended Sureshine and Blast.
- A total of 50 dentists recommended Sureshine.

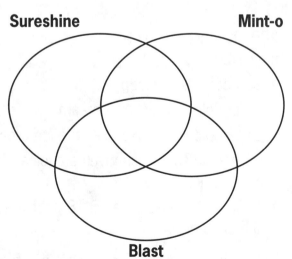

Logic Using a Venn Diagram

Use the Venn diagrams to display these results and answer the questions.

7. When asked which method of transportation 43 New Yorkers had used when traveling to Washington, D.C., in the last year, the following data was collected.

- 31 people said that they had traveled by train.
- 9 people said they had traveled by plane and train.
- 7 people said they had driven and gone by train.
- 4 people said they had only traveled by car.
- A total of 17 people said plane.
- Only 11 people said automobile.
- No one said they'd traveled by plane, train, and automobile.

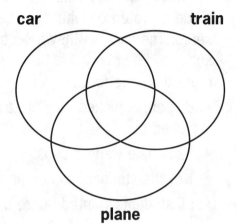

How many people said only train? _____

How many people said only plane? _____

How many people said only car? _____

Did anyone say plane and auto? _____

8. 200 students responded to a survey about desserts they liked.

- 20 people said just pie.
- 11 people said only ice cream.
- 31 people liked cake, pie, and ice cream equally.
- 59 people said when given a choice, they'd pick either cake or pie.
- 110 people liked cake with 8 people saying they like cake only.

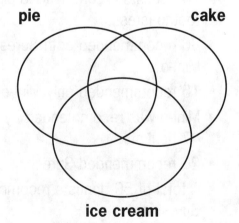

How many people said ice cream and pie? _____

How many people said both cake and ice cream? _____

Name _____

Logic Using a Venn Diagram

Use the Venn diagrams to display these results and answer the questions.

9. When asked which was more comfortable to wear to school, 31 students said that they liked to wear either sweats or jeans.

The same number of people said that they liked only jeans or said that they liked only sweats.

If a total of 59 people responded, how many people said jeans? _____

How many people said sweats? _____

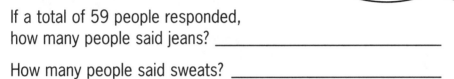

10. Afterschool students listed different activities that they did. Some students did more than one activity.

- 27 students had a music lesson, some sports activity, as well as religious school during the week.
- 39 students had both religious school and music lessons.
- 37 students had both religious school and some athletic activity.
- 30 more students had an athletic activity and a music lesson as the number of students who had a sport and religious school.
- A total of 84 students mentioned sports.
- A total of 51 students said religious school.
- 106 students responded.

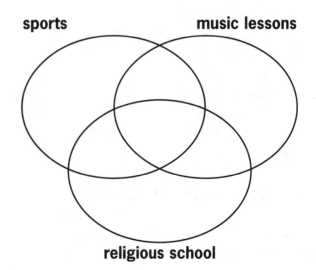

Answers

Poster Logic: Vegetable Gardens
1. Takani
2. Kim Yen
3. Eric
4. Paulo
5. Paulo
6. Takani
7. Kim Yen
8. Eric
9. Kim Yen
10. Eric
11. Takani
12. Kim Yen

Poster Logic: What Students Do With Their Allowance
1. Mr. Monroe's class
2. Ms. Saunder's class
3. Mr. Perez's class
4. Mr. Monroe's class
5. Ms. Ngyuen's class
6. Ms. Ngyuen's class
7. Ms. Saunder's class
8. Mr. Perez's class
9. Ms. Saunder's class
10. Mr. Monroe's class
11. Ms. Ngyen's class
12. Mr. Perez's class

Poster Logic: United States Flags
1. flag of 1818
2. flag of 1777
3. flag of 1930
4. flag of 1959
5. flag of 1777
6. flag of 1930
7. flag of 1959
8. flag of 1777
9. flag of 1959
10. flag of 1818
11. flag of 1930
12. flag of 1818

Poster Logic: Students' Savings
1. Sharnita
2. Jal
3. Brandon
4. Warren
5. Warren
6. Brandon
7. Warren
8. Jal
9. Brandon
10. Sharnita
11. Jal
12. Sharnita

Number Logic
1. 85
2. 46
3. 58
4. 24
5. 90
6. 491
7. 273
8. 169
9. 485
10. 230
11. 5,005
12. 7,234
13. 1,154
14. 2,354
15. 8,822
16. 17,359
17. 63,993
18. 97,053
19. 24,100
20. 40, 304

21. 0.25
22. 0.9
23. 0.178
24. 0.48
25. 0.067

Arithmetic Logic

1. $4 + 3 - 2 + 1 = 6$
2. $(9 \times 2) \div 6 + 1 = 4$ or
$(9 + 2) - 6 - 1 = 4$
3. $(7 + 9) \div 4 - 3 = 1$
4. $[(8 \div 4) \times 3] - 4 = 2$
5. $(1 \times 2) + 4 + 3 = 9$
6. $[(3 + 8) - 7] \times 2 = 8$
7. $12 \times 3 \div 9 + 8 = 12$
8. $[(15 \div 3) - 4] \times 7 = 7$ or
$[(15 + 3) - 4] - 7 = 7$
9. $1 + 4 + 6 - 8 = 3$
10. $2 \times 2 \times 2 - 2 = 6$
11. $(40 + 10) \times 2 - 30 = 70$
12. $20 - 10 + 60 + 20 = 90$
13. $90 \div 2 \div 5 + 1 = 10$
14. $60 \div 4 + 5 - 5 = 15$
15. $6 \times 5 \times 2 - 10 = 50$
16. $12 + 8 + 20 - 5 = 35$
17. $55 \times 2 - 10 + 20 = 120$
18. $75 - 25 + 15 - 10 = 55$
19. $80 \div 8 \times 2 \times 2 = 40$
20. $10 \times 10 \div 20 + 15 = 20$
21. $(136 - 20) \times 2 - 100 = 132$
22. $51 \div 3 + 12 - 1 = 28$
23. $164 \div 4 \times 2 + 27 = 109$
24. $88 \times 2 \div 4 - 10 = 34$
25. $100 \div 5 + 35 - 7 = 48$
26. $(0.75 - 0.30) \times 2 + 0.10 = 1.00$
27. $\frac{1}{2} - \frac{1}{6} + \frac{1}{5} = \frac{8}{15}$
28. $2 \times \frac{9}{10} - 1\frac{1}{3} = \frac{7}{15}$
29. $4 \times 0.25 + 0.10 - \frac{1}{2} = 0.6$
30. $[(\frac{2}{3} + \frac{1}{2}) - \frac{1}{4}] \times 2 = 1\frac{5}{6}$

Logic with a Matrix

1. Jessie: skim milk; Sandy: orange juice; Jamie: spring water
2. MaryBeth: python; Elizabeth: parrot; Beth: chameleon
3. Melissa: problem about Warren; John: problem about Matilda; Chau: problem about Evelyn
4. Doug: Ms. Carr; Matt: Mr. London; Jonah: Dr. Saunders; Jenny: Ms. Parsons
5. Grade 1: swimming pool; Grade 2: pond; Grade 3: ocean; Grade 4: lake
6. Peter: drama; Janice: science fiction; Andrew: comedy; Samuel: westerns
7. Marie: 12 km; Brian: 7 km; Sally: 10 km; Freddy: 11 km; Patricia: 5 km
8. Gordon: 4 hours, 40 minutes; Nikki: 3 hours, 45 minutes; Candi: 6 hours, 15 minutes; Stefanie: 5 hours, 20 minutes
9. Chau: Mountain Climb; Melinda: Tilt-a-Whirl; Hannah: Swamp Coaster; Petra: Ferris Wheel; Benita: Wild Grizzly
10. Camille: accountant; Josie: attorney; Beth: salon; Mike: teacher
11. Serena: *Charlie and the Chocolate Factory;* Matthew: *Tales of a Fourth Grade Nothing;* Jacob: *A Wrinkle in Time;* Dexter: *Stuart Little*
12. Felicity: December 26; Monroe: January 2; Belinda: July 5; Wyatt: February 15; Brook: March 18
13. Brian: $4782 + 999$; Henry: $1644 + 777$; Ernest: $827 + 699$; Chrisopher: $508 + 948$; Peter: $479 + 1356$.
14. Julie: 6 times; Kim: 9 times; J. M.: 11 times; Robbie: 2 times; Matthew: 7 times; David: 5 times
15. Mikhael: 523-8199; Sondrah: 356-1178; Charleen: 631-2140; Yolanda: 817-3624
16. Kevin: Sport, can stand on only two legs with the other two in the air; Earl: Bozo,

can jump over a barrel; Marvin: Harry, can jump through a hoop

17. Wanda: blue, Georgetown University; Rita: green, Brown University; Barb: red, Washington University; Greta: white, Rhode Island State University

18. First week: Baltimore; second week: Atlanta; third week: Charlotte; fourth week: Washington; fifth week: Omaha; sixth week: Kansas City; seventh week: Seattle; eighth week: Denver

Logic Using a Venn Diagram

1.

2.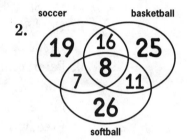

3.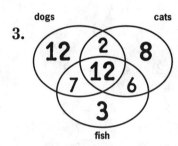

4.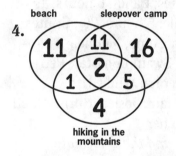

5.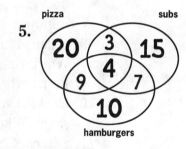

6.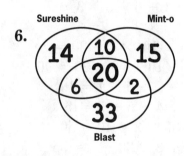

7.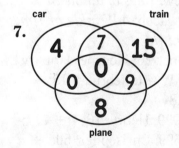

8.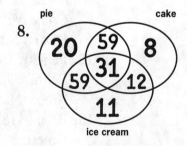

9.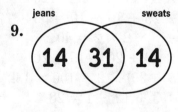

10.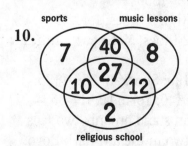